My Bl Words

Consultants

Ashley Bishop, Ed.D.

Sue Bishop, M.E.D.

Publishing Credits

Dona Herweck Rice, *Editor-in-Chief*

Robin Erickson, *Production Director*

Lee Aucoin, *Creative Director*

Sharon Coan, *Project Manager*

Jamey Acosta, *Editor*

Rachelle Cracchiolo, M.A.Ed., *Publisher*

Image Credits

cover Joop Hoek/Shutterstock; p.2 Nordling/Shutterstock; p.3 Noam Armonn/Shutterstock; p.5 irin-k/Shutterstock; p.6 Joop Hoek/Shutterstock; p.7 FikMik/Shutterstock; p.10 Valentyn Volkov/Shutterstock; back cover Valentyn Volkov/Shutterstock

Teacher Created Materials

5301 Oceanus Drive
Huntington Beach, CA 92649-1030
http://www.tcmpub.com

ISBN 978-1-4333-3974-5

© 2012 Teacher Created Materials, Inc.

Look at the blanket.

Where is the **bl**anket?

Look at black.

Where is black?

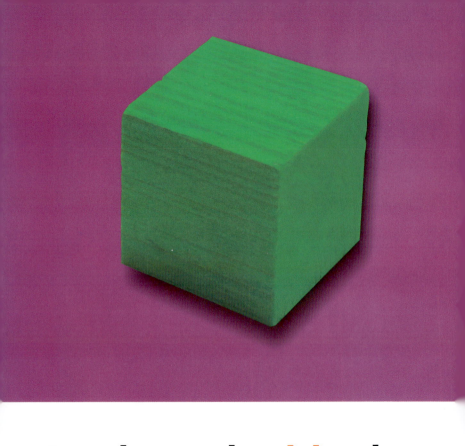

Look at the **block**.

Where are the blocks?

Look at **bl**ue.

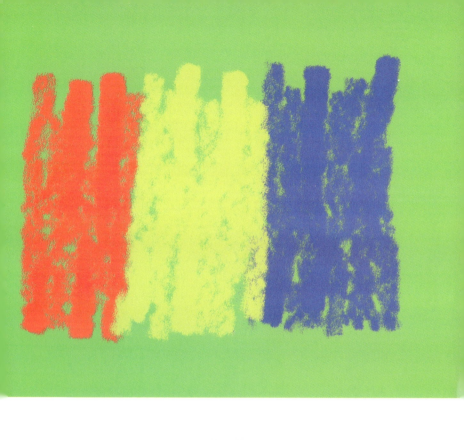

Where is blue?

Look at the **blueberries**

Glossary

 **bl**ack

 **bl**anket

 **bl**ock

 **bl**ue

 **bl**ueberries

Sight Words

Look at the Where is

Activities

- Read the book aloud to your child, pointing to the *bl* words. Help your child describe where the *bl* objects are found.

- Have your child color a paper with different shades of blue. Teach him or her the different names for blue, such as sky blue or navy blue.

- Buy some blueberries and have your child eat them for a snack. Discuss the color, texture, and flavor.

- Drape a blanket over a table so your child can play in a blanket house.

- Play a hinting game with objects that begin with *bl*. Begin by saying, "I see something black," and having your child guess what it is.

- Help your child think of a personally valuable word to represent the letters *bl*, such as *blast off*.